BALLOONS

BALLOONS

JON TREMAINE

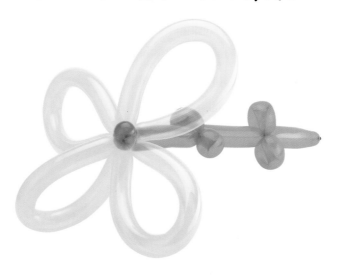

p

This is a Parragon Publishing Book

Parragon Publishing
Queen Street House
4 Queen Street
Bath BA1 1HE, UK

Copyright © Parragon 2001

Designed, produced, and packaged by
Stonecastle Graphics Limited

Design by Paul Turner and Sue Pressley
Photography by Roddy Paine
Edited by Philip de Ste. Croix
Diagrams by Jon Tremaine and
Malcolm Porter

ISBN 0-75255-687-8

Printed in China

WARNING – Children under
8 years of age can choke or
suffocate on uninflated or
broken balloons. Adult
supervision is required. Keep
uninflated balloons away
from children. Discard
broken balloons at once.

Contents

Introduction

Some people make a living by demonstrating balloon modeling and sculpture. Children's entertainers quickly realized the appeal and potential of these models and many top entertainers now include balloon modeling in their shows.

I cannot promise to make you into a superb entertainer. I can, however, promise to show you how to make some wonderful animals, birds, hats, and other surprising objects from balloons. In no time at all you will become the center of attention and an instant hit with all the kids in your neighborhood. The models all need practice to perfect but none of them is really difficult to make.

ABOUT BALLOONS

Until about 1960 balloon models were made by twisting several balloons together, but with the introduction of new, thinner, elongated balloons, a new art form was born. Dozens of models can now be made using just one balloon.

Most models are made from balloons called "260's." When fully inflated these balloons are approximately 2in (5cm) in diameter and 60in (150cm) long.

INFLATION

Some people have the natural knack of blowing up balloons and don't even have to think about it. Lucky them! Many others have great difficulty. Unless you are a "natural," I would suggest that you use a balloon pump to inflate your balloons. Simple pumps with special tapered nozzles which fit the thin necks of modeling balloons are readily available from most toyshops or good stationers.

STORAGE

Unfortunately balloons become brittle with age and they are then more prone to burst unexpectedly. It is essential that you look after them. Keep your balloons loosely packed in a cool place away from sunlight (the natural enemy of balloons). This will prolong the life of your balloons.

The odd balloon will still burst as you blow it up, but even the professional can't avoid this.

TWISTING

We twist the balloons in order to make bubbles of various sizes. This is easy to do. Pinch the balloon between the fingers and thumb of one hand and give the balloon two complete twists with the other hand. The second twist is to help lock the bubble into position.

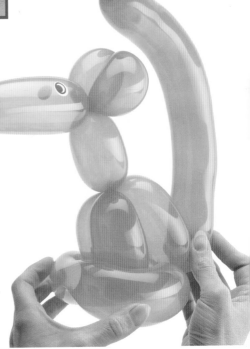

SAFETY FIRST!

Make sure that you instantly pick up all the pieces of any burst balloon and put them safely in the trash can so that they cannot end up in the mouths of small children or family pets. They could easily choke on these.

Never fully inflate your balloons. When you apply the various twists needed to make a model, the air must have somewhere to go, so an uninflated tip is always needed. The length of this will vary depending upon the number of twists that you require to make your model.

MARKER PENS AND STICKERS

A felt-tip permanent marker pen is useful for adding special features to your models. Try to find one that is specially designed to write on plastics, glass, and shiny surfaces, as the ink dries quickly with these types of marker. Other markers may tend to smudge and occasionally burst the balloons if you are not very careful. Your favorite stickers will look great on your balloon models too!

EYES, NOSES, AND THINGS!

Here are a few designs for eyes and other facial expressions. Use your marker pen or stickers to copy them onto the balloons.

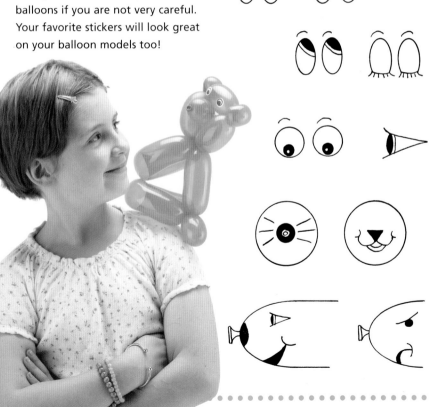

TYING OFF

It is surprising how many people can't tie a knot in an inflated balloon. It's easy when you know how! Let just a little of the air out first. This softens up the balloon and makes handling it easier.

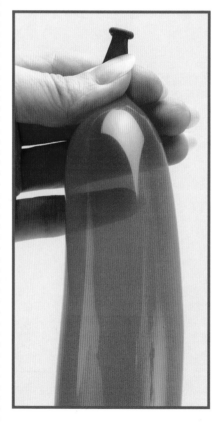

1. Hold the neck of the balloon between your left thumb and first and second fingers. Reach behind with your right hand and grip the lip of the balloon, pulling it down and back toward you around the fingers of your left hand.

2. Carry it across and grip it between the tips of your left first and second fingers.

If your balloons are warm they will be easy to work with – so keep your supply in your pocket. Your body heat will warm them up perfectly.

3. Now loop this end around the back of the neck of the balloon.

A COMMON PROBLEM SOLVED

You may find that, once made, the head of your model deflates within a few minutes. There are a couple of reasons why this could be happening. You may not be tying the knot tight enough – it is surprising how small an escape route the air requires. Alternatively you may be tying the knot too far down so weakening the wall of the balloon. The thickest and strongest part of the balloon is the neck. So that is the best spot for your knot.

That's all there is to it...but remember, practice makes perfect.

4. Pull the end through the loop you have made and your knot is complete.

Now let's get started. Over the page I show you how to make a simple model. It's an "all time favorite."

The Basic Hound Dog

This is often the first model that people ask for. It looks impressive and with practice it can *be* made in 30 seconds flat – and that includes the time spent blowing it up!

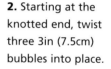

1. Inflate a balloon leaving about 3in (7.5cm) uninflated at the end.

2. Starting at the knotted end, twist three 3in (7.5cm) bubbles into place.

3. Pull the second bubble down so that it lines up with the third bubble and twist them around one another. You now have a head, nose, and two ears.

4. Twist three more 3in (7.5cm) bubbles.

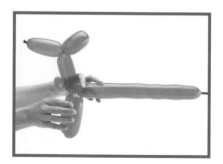

5. Bring the second of these down alongside the third bubble and twist them together. You have made the front legs.

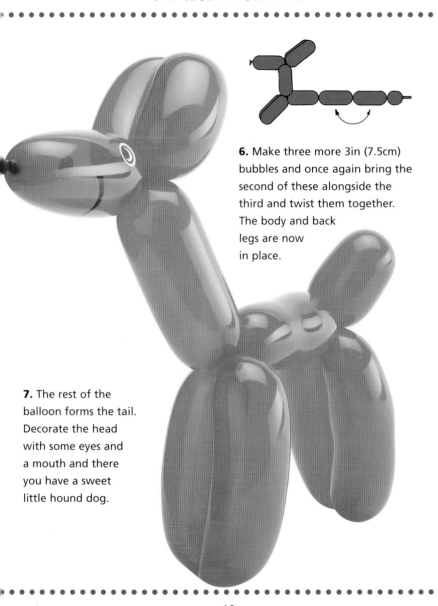

6. Make three more 3in (7.5cm) bubbles and once again bring the second of these alongside the third and twist them together. The body and back legs are now in place.

7. The rest of the balloon forms the tail. Decorate the head with some eyes and a mouth and there you have a sweet little hound dog.

Funny Bunny Rabbit

Two features identify a rabbit – its long ears and its bobtail.
This model captures both very well.

1. Inflate a
balloon leaving
a 3in (7.5cm) tip
uninflated.

2. Working from the balloon's neck
end, make a 3in (7.5cm) bubble
followed by two 6in (15cm) bubbles

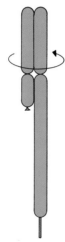

4. Make two 3in (7.5cm) bubbles –
align them and twist them together.
These are the front legs.

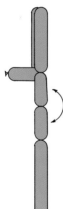

5. Make another 3in
(7.5cm) bubble (this
forms the body).

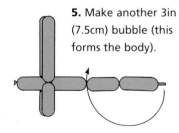

3. Bring the two 6in
(15cm) bubbles together
and twist them around
one another. These are
the rabbit's ears.

6. Make another 3in (7.5cm) bubble
(one back leg).

7. Squeeze air into the remaining balloon tip to inflate it. Double this last bubble back – crossing it over the last joint so that it overlaps by about 1in (2.5cm).

9. Tuck the front legs down between the back legs and the cute little rabbit will sit up for you.

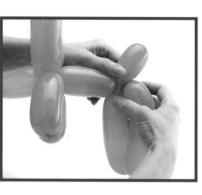

8. Twist the back legs around a couple of times to lock them into position and you will have formed the rabbit's back legs and distinguishing bobtail!

Cute Teddy Bear

It took me quite a while to master how to form the head of this model so I have gone to a lot of trouble to make its construction as clear as possible so that you find it easier than I did. It is not really difficult – just a little fiddly. Persevere as it's well worth it! The finished teddy bear is a delight.

1. Inflate a balloon but leave about 5in (12.5cm) uninflated.

2. You must now make a chain of seven bubbles measuring as follows: 1in, 1in, 2in, 1in, 1.5in, 1in, 2in (2.5cm, 2.5cm, 5cm, 2.5cm, 4cm, 2.5cm, 5cm). The tricky bit is to keep some of the twists from unraveling. Don't worry if the first 1in (2.5cm) bubble unravels. You can always re-make it later.

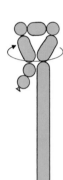

3. Bring the two 2in (5cm) bubbles together and give them a twist where shown.

4. You now perform two ear twists. This is a new type of twist that is used extensively by balloon sculptors.

Grip an ear bubble firmly and pull it upward a little – then give it a twist (I always think of a naughty little boy as I do this!). This has the effect of isolating the ear bubble on the outside of the face. Do ear twists on both top 1in (2.5cm) bubbles.

5. Now push the very first balloon through the gap in the middle of the face. The knotted end acts as the bear's nose. Draw eyes on the face.

8. Make a 2in (5cm) bubble (the body). Make another 4in (10cm) loop and twist it around the last joint to form the back legs.

9. This leaves a little tail bubble.

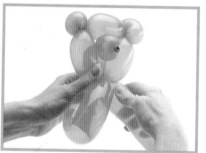

6. Make a 1in (2.5cm) bubble (the neck).

7. Now make a 4in (10cm) loop and twist it around the joint (the front legs).

Ollie Octopus

This spectacular creature is probably the easiest of all the balloon models to make. You will need four 260's and one ordinary round balloon – all of the same color. Red looks very good.

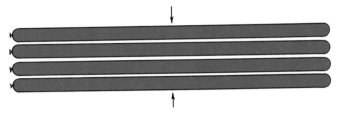

1. Fully inflate the four 260's.

2. Line them up side by side and locate the center.

3. Grip all four balloons and twist them together. Hey presto! You have made the eight tentacles.

4. Inflate the round balloon and tie it off.

5. Wrap the neck of the round balloon around the center joint of the tentacles a couple of times.

6. Apart from decorating the head with eyes and a happy smile – that's it!

Sammy Spider

A Halloween horror! Make several and hang them in dark corners with a few of your Bat-mobiles (see page 44). Your friends will be well spooked!

1. Follow the procedure for making Ollie Octopus, but this time use dark-colored balloons. Black is obviously the best color. Twist an extra bubble at the end of each leg to make a foot, and decorate your spider with a scary face and fangs. Help!

Dumbo the Jumbo

This cute little chap looks pretty much like that famous flying elephant from the Walt Disney cartoon that we all know and love.

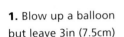

1. Blow up a balloon but leave 3in (7.5cm) of it uninflated.

2. Make a 1in (2.5cm) bubble followed by two 1.5in (4cm) bubbles.

3. Twist the two 1.5in (4cm) bubbles together to make the back legs. The first bubble is the tail.

4. Make another 1in (2.5cm) bubble and two more 1.5in (4cm) bubbles.

5. Twist the two 1.5in (4cm) bubbles together. You have made the body and the front legs.

6. Make a 6in (15cm) bubble and fold it in half – twisting the joints to fix it. You have made the first ear.

8. The rest of the balloon forms the elephant's trunk. Stroke it a few times to make it curve upward and draw some eyes to complete Dumbo the Jumbo.

7. Make another 6in (15cm) bubble and form the other ear in the same way.

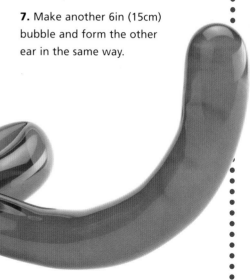

Mighty Mouse

Nine bubbles, all the same size, a couple of twists and you have made your cat's favorite! Try making several in different colors. Don't forget to draw on the whiskers, eyes, and mouth.

1. Inflate about half of your balloon. The uninflated part will act as the tail when your model is complete.

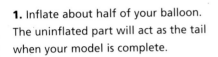

2. Make three 1.5in (4cm) bubbles.

3. Twist the second and third bubbles together and you will have made the head and two ears.

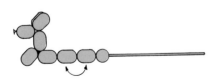

4. Make three more 1.5in (4cm) bubbles.

5. Twist the second and third together and you have made the neck and front legs.

6. Make three more 1.5in (4cm) bubbles. Twist the second and third together and you have made the body and back legs.

7. This leaves a small bubble and a long thin tail. That rounds off your marvelous mouse.

Rudi Reindeer

This wonderful model uses two balloons – a red one for the deer and a green one for its magnificent antlers. It's fun and easy to make.

The Deer:

1. Inflate the red balloon leaving a 2in (5cm) uninflated tip.

2. Make a 2in (5cm) bubble at the knotted end of the balloon. This is the head.

3. Twist another 2in (5cm) bubble to form the neck.

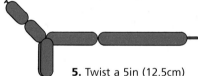

5. Twist a 5in (12.5cm) bubble to form the body.

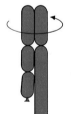

4. For the front legs, make two 3in (7.5cm) bubbles. Pull the second one down so that it lies alongside the first one and twist them together at the joint to secure them.

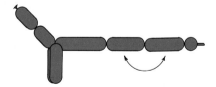

6. For the back legs, make two more 3in (7.5cm) bubbles and twist them together just as you did when you made the front legs.

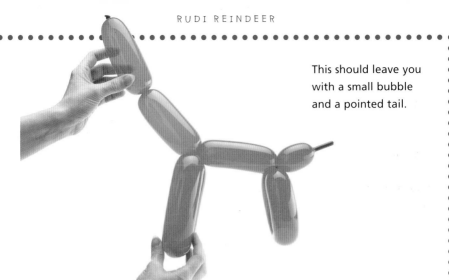

This should leave you with a small bubble and a pointed tail.

The Antlers:
8. Inflate the green balloon leaving about a 1in (2.5cm) uninflated tip.

9. From the knot end make a string of three 2in (5cm) bubbles.

10. Line up the second and third bubbles and twist them together. You will now have three "branches" on one antler.

11. Put three 2in (5cm) bubbles on the other end of the balloon.

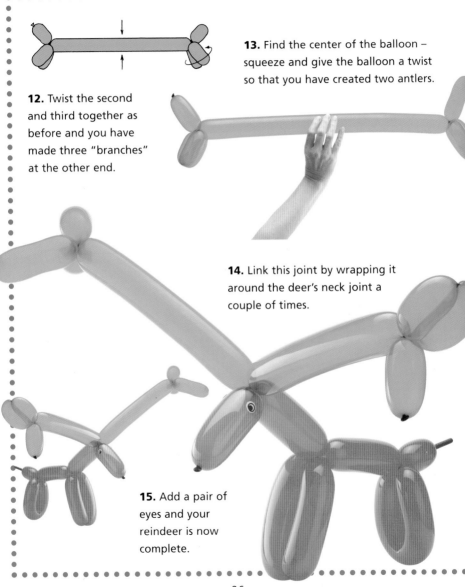

13. Find the center of the balloon – squeeze and give the balloon a twist so that you have created two antlers.

12. Twist the second and third together as before and you have made three "branches" at the other end.

14. Link this joint by wrapping it around the deer's neck joint a couple of times.

15. Add a pair of eyes and your reindeer is now complete.

Rocking Horse

Balloon sculptors have produced many elaborate versions of rocking horses. By skillful means they are able to recreate manes, reins, saddles, and even mounted riders!

Our model is a lot less complicated than that but I am sure that you will love it. You need two 260's – a light-colored one for the horse and a dark-colored one for the rocker.

The Horse:

In this design we need to, create a model with a long face, small ears, and long legs.

1. Inflate your balloon leaving a tip of about 3in (7.5cm).

2. Make a 3in (7.5cm) bubble (this will be the head) followed by two 1in (2.5cm) bubbles.

3. Twist these two bubbles together to make the ears.

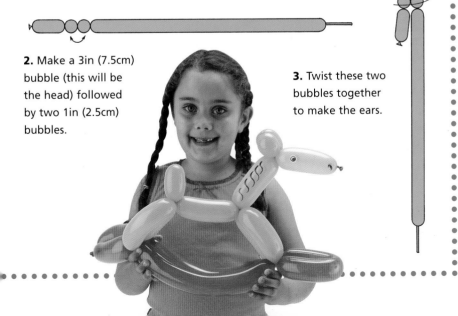

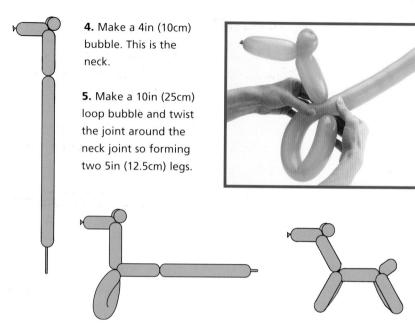

4. Make a 4in (10cm) bubble. This is the neck.

5. Make a 10in (25cm) loop bubble and twist the joint around the neck joint so forming two 5in (12.5cm) legs.

6. Make a 4in (10cm) bubble to represent the body of the horse.

7. Make another 10in (25cm) loop bubble to create the back legs. You are left with a small tail.

The Rocker:

8. Inflate your balloon leaving only a 0.5in (12mm) tip uninflated.

9. Fold the balloon in half and tie the neck knot and the small, uninflated tip together.

10. Twist a 4in (10cm) double bubble at one end. Force it through the loop of the front legs and push the joint downward so that the legs of the horse stretch over the joint and hold the balloon in place.

11. Twist a 4in (10cm) double bubble on the other end of the rocker. Push this through the back legs of the horse and fix it into position in the same way.

12. Finish by adding eyes and drawing in the mane. Isn't that terrific?

Groovy Giraffe

The shape of our 260 balloons just cries out for them
to be used for a model with a long neck. The giraffe (in balloon
terms) is a direct descendant of the hound dog!
Use a brown or yellow balloon.

1. Inflate your balloon and leave a
3in (7.5cm) tip.

2. Make a 3in
(7.5cm) bubble at
the knot end of
the balloon. This
is the head.

4. Twist a 12in (30cm) bubble
to form the animal's very long
neck.

3. Make two 1in
(2.5cm) bubbles
for the ears and
secure them with
ear twists.

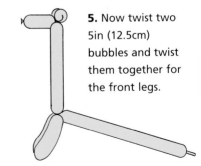

5. Now twist two
5in (12.5cm)
bubbles and twist
them together for
the front legs.

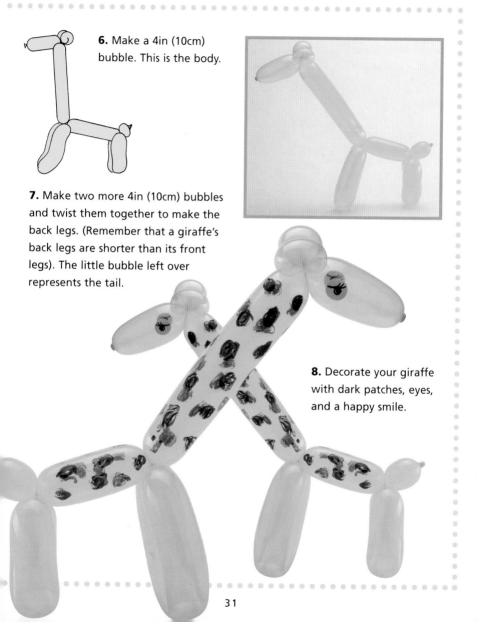

6. Make a 4in (10cm) bubble. This is the body.

7. Make two more 4in (10cm) bubbles and twist them together to make the back legs. (Remember that a giraffe's back legs are shorter than its front legs). The little bubble left over represents the tail.

8. Decorate your giraffe with dark patches, eyes, and a happy smile.

31

The Lion King

Use an orange balloon for this model. It is similar to the hound dog – but watch out because the head is a little different.

1. Blow up a balloon leaving a 3in (7.5cm) tip uninflated.

2. Make three 4in (10cm) bubbles.

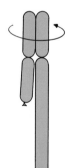

3. Twist the last two 4in (10cm) bubbles together.

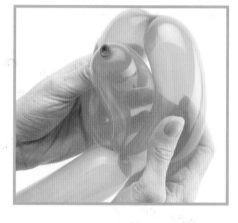

4. Now push the first 4in (10cm) bubble between the two ear bubbles until about half of it projects. You have completed the lion's head with its magnificent wraparound mane.

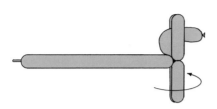

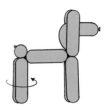

5. Make two 4in (10cm) bubbles and twist them together for the front legs.

6. Make a 4in (10cm) bubble for the body and follow this with two 3.5in (9cm) bubbles. Twist these together to make the back legs.

7. This should leave you with a little tail bubble. Add some eyes to round off your King of the Jungle.

Sammy Sealion

When we think of a sealion, we usually think of its big back flippers and its ability to balance a ball skillfully on its nose. This one-balloon model achieves all that. We will make this model from back to front.

1. Inflate the balloon and then let all the air out again – then re-inflate the balloon leaving a small, uninflated tip. (The point of deflating the balloon is to make it a little softer and easier to work with.)

2. Make a 14in (35cm) bubble at the pointed end.

3. Bend it into a circle and wrap the uninflated point around the joint to secure it.

4. Find the center of the circle and push it in to make a figure eight shape. Twist the two "flippers" you have made to secure them.

5. Leaving sufficient of the balloon for a body, twist an "S" bend further down the balloon. Find the center of the "S" bend and twist the three thicknesses together to make sealion's little front "flippers."

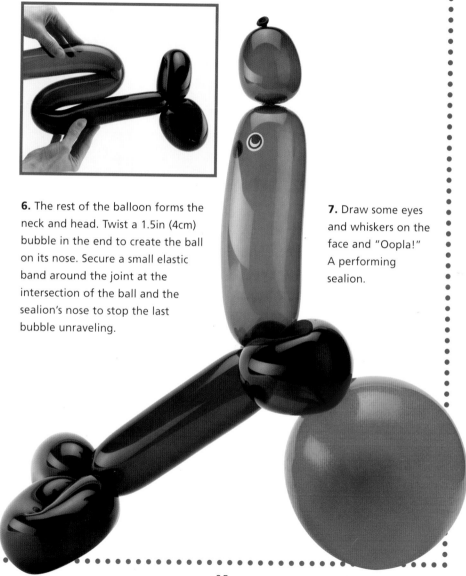

6. The rest of the balloon forms the neck and head. Twist a 1.5in (4cm) bubble in the end to create the ball on its nose. Secure a small elastic band around the joint at the intersection of the ball and the sealion's nose to stop the last bubble unraveling.

7. Draw some eyes and whiskers on the face and "Oopla!" A performing sealion.

Cyril Squirrel

My experience as a party entertainer has shown me that this is one of my most popular models. We need to create a long curved bushy tail, little ears, small front legs, and longer back legs to capture the look of a squirrel.

1. Inflate your balloon leaving a 2.5in (6.5cm) uninflated tip.

2. From the neck end, twist a 2.5in (6.5cm) head.

3. Now make two 1in (2.5cm) ear bubbles and twist them together.

4. Twist a 2.5in (6.5cm) neck bubble.

5. Make two 2in (5cm) front leg bubbles and twist them together.

6. Make a 2.5in (6.5cm) body bubble.

7. Make two 3in (7.5cm) back leg bubbles and twist them together. You should be left with a tail about 12in (30cm) long.

8. Push the front legs between the back legs to make the squirrel sit up. Curl the tail upward and over the head in a squirrel's characteristic pose.

Hummingbird

The hovering position of a typical hummingbird and its long beak for extracting nectar from flowers are caught in this delightful model. Add some eyes and the impression is complete.

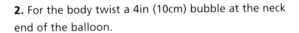

1. Inflate a balloon leaving a 2in (5cm) uninflated tip. This tip will eventually become the bird's long beak.

2. For the body twist a 4in (10cm) bubble at the neck end of the balloon.

3. A 3in (7.5cm) bubble just behind the uninflated beak will make the head.

4. The wings are created by folding the very long bubble in a loop and twisting both end joints together.

5. Press the center of the loop down until it reaches the body and neck joints. Hold everything together firmly.

6. Take one of the wings you have just formed and twist it around a couple of times to lock everything into place.

7. Add eyes on each side of the head. That's it. Subtle, quick, and simple.

Buzzy Buzzy Bee

This fine model is very similar to the humming bird. It could just as well double as a wasp. (Ouch.) It's best to use a yellow balloon on which you can mark some black stripes.

1. Inflate a balloon leaving a 2in (5cm) uninflated tip. This tip will become the bee's sting.

2. For the head twist a 3in (7.5cm) bubble at the knot end of the balloon.

3. The body is made from a 4in (10cm) bubble formed just behind the uninflated end.

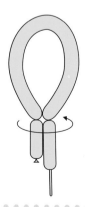

4. Now for the wings: fold the very long bubble in a loop and twist both end joints around one another.

5. Press the center of the loop down until it reaches the body and neck joints. Hold everything together firmly.

6. Take one wing and twist it around a couple of times to lock everything into place.

7. For the finishing touches, add eyes on each side of the head and paint bold black stripes around the bee's body.

Q: What goes "Zzub, Zzub, Zzub?"
A: A bee flying backward!

41

Swinging Parrot

This little fellow looks superb. The beak, head, and tail are cleverly defined while the bird actually sits on its perch.

1. Inflate a balloon. Leave about 1in (2.5cm) uninflated.

2. From the neck end make a 1in (2.5cm) bubble (the beak) – then a 1.5in (4cm) bubble (the head).

3. Pull the beak bubble down to line up with the joint of the head bubble.

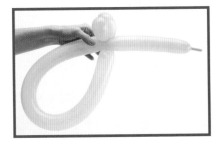

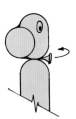

4. Twist the little knotted piece around this joint a couple of times to fix the head and beak section.

5. Loop the rest of the balloon around and overlap it across the joint by about 10in (25cm). This section will make the tail.

6. Press down at the joint, twist and pull the 10in (25cm) tail over and down behind.

7. The next move "makes" the body and at the same time makes the swing smaller. Press inward to bring both sides of the swing down the sides of the tail.

8. About 5in to 6in (12.5-15cm) down, grip all three thicknesses together and give them a single twist.

9. You now have a parrot hanging upside down from the perch! Simply revolve the body and tail until the parrot is sitting happily astride the swing. Decorate the bird with eyes, beak, and nostrils. Pretty Polly!

Batty Bat

A bat has enormous wings and very sensitive, large ears so we must try to capture these in our model. Choose a black balloon for the best effect. You could make several bats and hang them from the ceiling in your bedroom. Very spooky – especially at night!

1. Blow up a balloon but leave about 2in (5cm) uninflated.

2. For the head, make a 1.5in (4cm) bubble.

3. The ears are created from two 1in (2.5cm) bubbles.

4. Give them both an ear twist (as previously explained on page 16).

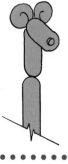

5. Make a 1.5in (4cm) bubble for the neck.

6. Now we have to make the large wings. Make a 12in (30cm) bubble and, after bending it in half, link the last joint with the previous one – which is just beneath the neck – by giving it a couple of twists.

7. Make another 12in (30cm) bubble. Bend it around and secure it in the same place with a couple of twists.

8. This should leave you with about a 1.5in (4cm) bubble at the end which is the body. Add a couple of eyes and your vampire bat is ready to fly.

Jon's Swans

I always strive for simplicity. To make this attractive swan you need only make three bubbles! What could be simpler than that?

1. Use a white or yellow balloon. Leave about 1.5in (4cm) uninflated. This will form the beak.

2. Working from the neck end of the balloon, make three 6in (15cm) bubbles.

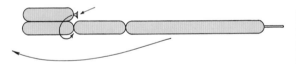

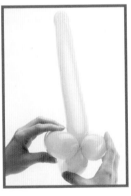

3. Fold the first one on top of the second one and twist them together by wrapping the knotted end around the joint.

4. Swing the next bubble and the rest of the balloon beneath these two.

5. Force the joint of this last balloon between the other two balloons and the neck section will stay in place.

46

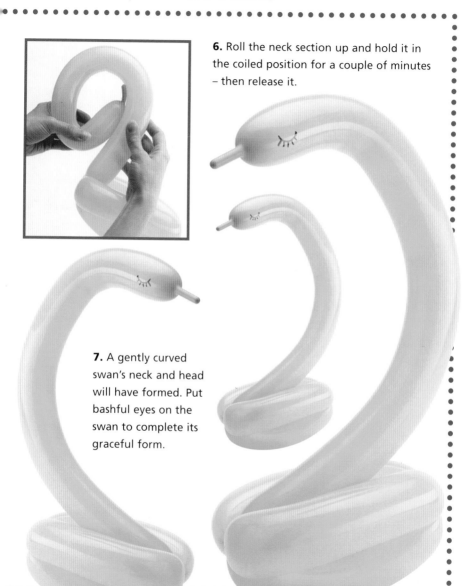

6. Roll the neck section up and hold it in the coiled position for a couple of minutes – then release it.

7. A gently curved swan's neck and head will have formed. Put bashful eyes on the swan to complete its graceful form.

Deadly Ray Gun

A fine "weapon" for the over-active child! This is almost as quick to make as the Viking sword (see page 64) – so you could arm a whole battalion of kids in almost no time at all.

1. Inflate a balloon leaving about a 1in (2.5cm) tip uninflated.

2. From the neck end make a 3in (7.5cm) bubble.

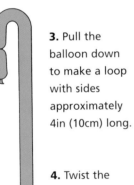

3. Pull the balloon down to make a loop with sides approximately 4in (10cm) long.

4. Twist the loop to fix it in position

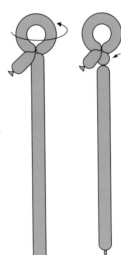

5. Make a small 1in (2.5cm) bubble.

6. Now make another 4in (10cm) loop.

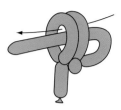

8. Thread the rest of the balloon through the two loops leaving a little behind to act as the gun's handle.

7. Twist it to fix it as before.

9. Straighten out the ray gun's barrel and look for the nearest alien to zap!

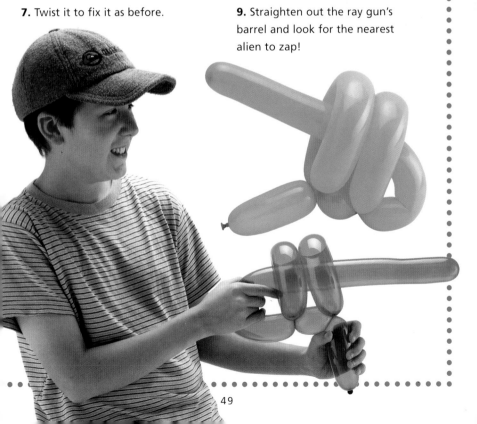

High Flier

This is another balloon model that most boys love. It is very simple to make and in the process we will learn to do an apple twist.

1. Inflate your balloon but leave about 2in (5cm) uninflated at the end.

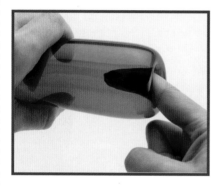

2. Hold the balloon a little way behind the knotted end with your left hand. With you right index finger push the knotted end back into the balloon as far as you can.

3. Grip the knot through the balloon with your left finger and thumb. Give the bubble a few twists until it stays in place. You will now have a 2in (5cm) bubble with a concave end. This is known as the apple twist.

4. Starting at the bubble end, make three bends (not twists) each 8in (20cm) long, like a letter "S."

5. Find the center and give the three thicknesses a twist. This forms the aircraft's wings. Take care to pinch the exact center, otherwise your wings will be of uneven lengths. Each wing will be approximately 4in (10cm) long.

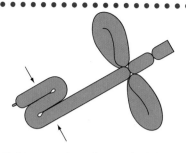

6. Move to the other end of the balloon and make another "S" bend – say about 6in (15cm) long this time. Find the center, press and then twist the three sections together as before. You have now formed the rear tailplane and horizontal stabilizers.

7. Decorate your airplane with stickers if you have some, and you are ready for take-off.

Mother's Day Flowers

This bouquet of balloon tulips will come as a nice surprise for
your mother on her "special" day. Use as many different colors as
you can lay your hands on. You will also need a
drinking straw for each bloom.

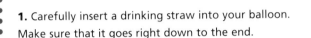

1. Carefully insert a drinking straw into your balloon.
Make sure that it goes right down to the end.

2. Inflate about 4in (10cm) of your
balloon and then tie it off.

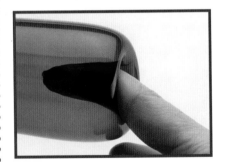

3. You are now going to do an apple
twist in this end. (That's the twist that
we have just learned for the airplane,
remember?) Hold the balloon just
behind the bubble in your left hand
and push the knot into the balloon
with your right index finger.

4. Grip this knot between your left
finger and thumb when you can and
then give the bubble a couple of
twists to secure it.

5. Carefully ease up the drinking straw so that the end of it sits just behind the bulb of your tulip. It acts as a flower stem.

6. Make lots of tulips and display them in a vase for best effect. Use lots of different colors for a really spectacular bouquet.

Giant Sunflower

This is fun to make. You will need two yellow balloons for the petals and one green balloon for the leaves and stem.

1. Blow up one of the yellow balloons leaving just a small section at the end uninflated.

2. Make it into a circle by tying the pointed end to the neck end.

3. Find the center and press it down to meet the knots.

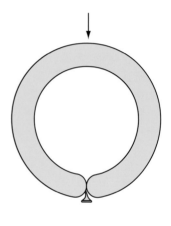

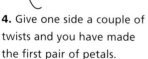

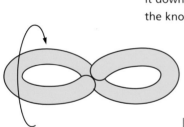

4. Give one side a couple of twists and you have made the first pair of petals.

5. Do the same with the second yellow balloon and then twist the two separate petal sections together.

6. Inflate the green balloon leaving about 1in (2.5cm) uninflated.

7. Make an "S" bend a little way up the stem, find its center and twist the three thicknesses together so forming two leaves.

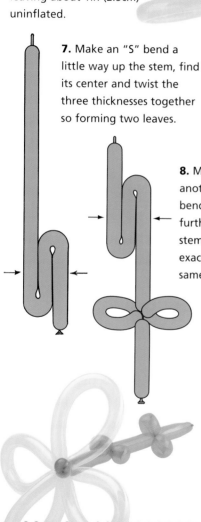

8. Make another "S" bend a little further up the stem and do exactly the same thing.

9. Form a 3in (7.5cm) bubble at the end and wrap this joint around the central joint of the yellow petals so holding the flower head in position. Your gigantic sunflower is complete.

55

Flower Power Hat

This is a very novel party hat and it's so easy to make. You need three balloons – one green and two yellow.

The Headband and Flower Stem:

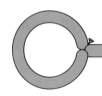

1. Inflate the green balloon fully. Measure how far it is around your head (usually between 20in and 24in, 50cm-60cm) and make a bubble this long.

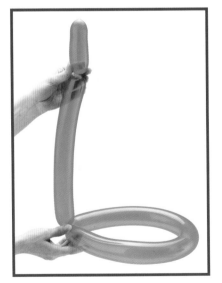

2. Bend this bubble into a circle and wrap some of the knotted end around the joint a few times to fix the headband.

3. Point the rest of the balloon upward and make a 3in (7.5cm) bubble on the end.

The Petals:

4. Inflate one of the yellow balloons and tie it into a circle.

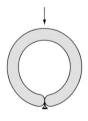

5. Find its center – push it down to the knotted joint and give one side a couple of twists to secure the two petals.

6. Do the same with the other yellow balloon.

7. Twist the two sets of petals onto the stem of the flower at the joint of the bubble at its end. There you have a crazy floral hat that's ideal for any party.

White Swan Hat

One of the simplest balloon hats to make is this swan.
It takes only a minute to make but will give hours of pleasure to
a child. Use a white 260 balloon.

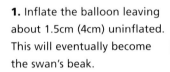

1. Inflate the balloon leaving
about 1.5cm (4cm) uninflated.
This will eventually become
the swan's beak.

2. Size the hat by wrapping it
around the head of the person
who is going to wear it and
twisting the knot into the joint
to fix the headband.

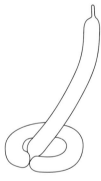

3. Push the head
and neck section
of the swan into
the headband
circle.

4. Roll the neck
section up and hold it
in the coiled position
for a couple of
minutes – then
release it.

5. This forms the elegant curve of the swan's neck. Decorate the head with eyes to complete a very effective swan hat.

Crowning Glory

This zany head-dress will cause quite a stir. You won't find an Easter Parade hat to beat it! You will need two different colored 260's and an ordinary round balloon of a third color.

1. Inflate both 260's leaving just a little uninflated tip at the ends.

2. Now – this is a bit tricky – make a 2in (5cm) bubble at the knotted end of both. Lie them side by side as shown. Note that the bubbles are pointing in opposite directions.

3. Wrap each bubble around the body of the opposite balloon. Where? Well, when opened up, the loop that you have just formed will be the headband of our crown – so you may have to fiddle about a bit to find the right proportions. Just make sure that both balloons have the same length sections left over.

4. Find the midpoint of the left-over sections and twist the balloons together at that point.

5. Make 2in (5cm) bubbles on the ends of what is left and wrap the bubble joints around the centers of the opposite-colored balloons.

6. Inflate your round balloon and, after knotting it, stretch the knot and wrap the rubber around the top joint of the crown a couple of times. It will stay in position.

7. Time for the coronation and this is the jewel in the crown!

Mad Martian Hat

This is a fun hat to make. It has been a great favorite with all the youngsters that I have entertained over the years.
You need two balloons.

1. Inflate both balloons leaving a 6in (15cm) tip uninflated at the end of each. This is important. Put them side by side and tie the two knots together.

2. Position the knots at the back of the wearer's head and bring the two balloons around the head – one on each side – to size the headband accurately.

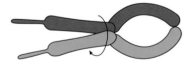

3. Remove the balloons and twist them together at the marked point.

4. Twist a 4in (10cm) double bubble on each balloon. This brings the antennae into an upright position.

5. Squeeze a little air down to the uninflated ends to create little 1in (2.5cm) bubbles at the very tips.

Earthling...take me
to your Leader!

Viking Sword

An all-time favorite with boys! They can have vicious sword fights without coming to any harm. This must be the easiest model in the book to create – just three folds and a twist and you've got it made!

1. Inflate your balloon leaving just about 0.5in (12mm) uninflated to allow for expansion at the end.

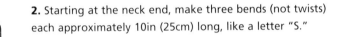

2. Starting at the neck end, make three bends (not twists) each approximately 10in (25cm) long, like a letter "S."

3. Grip all three thicknesses and, finding the center, twist them all together.

4. Tweak the hilt and the sword handle into place.

5. Run the "blade" through your hand to straighten it and your sword is complete. On guard!